I0485874

FREAKS

An art project by Robert Priseman
With essay by Ewen Speed

SEABROOK PRESS

CONTENTS

Writing

Drawings

Thanks

AN INTRODUCTION

NORMAL

In his book *Going Sane* (2005) the psychoanalyst Adam Phillips observed that sanity is usually "referred to without its meaning ever being spelled out", arguing that whilst insanity can be subdivided into many different clinical categories, sanity itself is only ever defined as the absence of madness. In otherwords, the rational mind is viewed only as an abstract concept, a kind of Platonic ideal which remains somehow disconnected from the 'real' world.

Just as our mental 'normality' can only truly be appreciated as a lack of strange behaviour, so too can our understanding of physical ordinariness only really be grasped as a lack of bodily deformity. In this way we may identify normalcy as existing in the absence of imperfection. 'Normal' exists in the same sphere as 'sane' and 'perfect', they are concepts which act to define the very essence of who we are as people, yet they strangely appear to be 'beyond human'. Perhaps this is because an absence appears to indicate that something of our being is missing. Yet to sense definitions in terms of theoretical concepts which we can't see is to place our thinking in the territory of the unreal; to locate it in a world which is beyond our physical touch and in the realm of perfection.

When we look historically we find many examples of how people who suffered with physical disabilities were treated as social outcasts, from the 'freaks' who worked as side-show performers in Europe and the USA to the victims of Nazi Germany's T4 Euthanasia Programme. Isolated, stared at and murdered, individuals who displayed a marked deviation from the 'norm' in the past have often been treated as though they themselves were somehow less than human. Yet perhaps when we look more closely at people like Prince Randian or Frieda Pushnik, people who were born without limbs and who both worked as side-show performers, what we find are men and women of strength, courage and determination. Their ability to overcome the immense difficulties which the randomness of life threw their way seems to mark them out as somehow 'ultra' human. For despite having been born without arms and legs Prince Randian learnt to speak five languages, was able to paint, write and shave himself. He married and together with his wife had four daughters and a son. Frieda Pushnik was also similarly able, yet her limbs had been severed in the womb as a result of a botched appendectomy. Despite this she never resented her condition and never wished to sue the attending doctor for malpractice, saying "I never said, 'Why me?' That would be a wasted emotion. You can ruin your life like that".

Perhaps a reason for some of the social cruelties and inequalities which have been enacted on those with a physical disability in the past lies in a sense that when we notice a significant deviation from the 'norm' in someone else it serves to remind us that 'normal', like 'perfection' is an abstract concept from which we all fall short. This is a gap the plastic surgery industry seeks to exploit. Yet perhaps we can see that the pursuit of perfection is in itself a kind of insanity, because it represents a goal which can never be realised. Maybe real sanity is found when we embrace our imperfections and appreciate ourselves for who we really are; all too human, flaws and all.

Robert Priseman 2015

ON FREAKS, FREAKERY AND POLICING THE CENTRE

ON FREAKS FREAKERY AND POLICING THE CENTRE

What Robert Priseman demonstrates in this project are historical processes and practices around representations of disability, for make no mistake, the 'freaks' represented here would be identified as disabled in modern parlance. Freaks and freakery have an ambiguous history, simultaneously regarded as fascinating and abhorrent. Elizabeth Grosz, in an essay titled 'intolerable ambiguity: freaks as/at the limit'1 describes how the idea of the freak appeals directly to "our most fundamental categories of self-definition and boundaries dividing self from otherness". Similarly, Michel Foucault talks about the idea of 'otherness', highlighting how it operates as a binary logic, dividing society into two groups;

"...them and us, the unjust and the just, the masters and those who must obey them, the rich and the poor, the mighty and those who have to work in order to live, those who invade lands and those who tremble before them, the despots and the groaning people, the men of today's law and those of the homeland of the future."2

These ideas of difference between two groups are central to the social, cultural and political processes around freaks and freakery. Grosz argues that the freak fulfils a role for the viewer in confirming them as "bounded, belonging to a "proper" social category. The viewers horror lies in the recognition that this monstrous being is at the heart of his or her own identity, for it is all that must be ejected or abjected from self-image to make the bounded, category-obeying self possible." When viewed in this context, the freak functions to assert categories of membership which people seem to be either excluded from or included in – a society wide split between an in-group and an out-group. It is this aspect of freaks and freakery that I want to discuss in this essay.

In order to do this I want to look at the role that freaks and freakery have played, and indeed continue to play, in defining not the margins, but the centre – the bounded belonging, category-obeying centre – and how this tells us much more about the social, cultural and political values and norms of that 'centre' than it does about those excluded to the periphery.

In terms of contrasting the centre to the periphery, and what this might reveal, consider the othering of disability inherent in the global rise of eugenics and in particular the development of eugenic state policies in Nazi Germany. Robert Priseman's previous project 'Nazi Gas Chambers: From Memory to History' detailed the rise of the T4 Killing Centres, as precursors to the horrors of the concentration camps. The development of these T4 Killing Centres was predicated upon social processes that identified the sick and disabled as a burden upon the broader population. In 1933 the Law for the Prevention of Genetically Diseased Offspring (the so-called sterilisation law) was passed, which effectively split German society into the 'sick' (and burdensome) and the 'healthy', with the state able to forcibly sterilise those deemed burdensome, such that their progeny could not effect a similar burden on the state. From this precedent, in 1939, the national euthanasia programme was initiated, whereby physicians inspecting children deemed to be 'genetically unhealthy' were empowered to grant the child euthanasia. Within a year, the Committee for the Scientific Treatment of Severe, Genetically Determined Illnesses required all health professionals delivering a child with congenital deformities such as "idiocy or Mongolism, microcephaly or hydrocephaly, deformities of any kind, malformation of the head or spina bifida, or crippling deformities such as spastics to register that child with the local health authorities – to clarify certain scientific questions in areas of congenital deformity and mental retardation"[3]. More than 5000 children were killed as part of this programme. And the scope of the legislation extended beyond children. By August 1941, 70,000 patients from more than 100 German hospitals had been killed. Three scientific/medical organisations were created to plan for the extermination of all of Germany's mental patients and handicapped children. Of the 283,000 people identified as possible 'mercy killings', approximately 75,000 were marked to die. The euthanasia programmes, which 'othered' whole swathes of the population, created the conditions of possibility for the final solution. The social norms established around the 'othering' of disabled groups led to the 'othering' of other non-medically defined groups such as Jews, communists, homosexuals, Gypsies, Slavs, and prisoners of war.

Many of these state policies were underpinned by notions of eugenics, and not just in Nazi Germany. In the late 1800s and early 1900s eugenics was a respected science. Francis Galton, the British founder of the eugenics movement was the nephew of Charles Darwin. It was predicated on a general principle that human progress could only be ensured through national breeding programmes designed to increase the number of children born to the educated, intelligent, and accomplished upper classes. Eugenicists also felt it was necessary to discourage the birth of children among poor and handicapped lower classes, arguing that it was science, not religion nor philosophy that would direct humanity toward a biological, social and moral utopia. The utility of the Victorian freak is plain to see in terms of the role that this category of human being could play in helping to define both the centre and the margins of this burgeoning new (pseudo) science.

Just what were the margins that these freaks were intended to identify, what were the social, political and cultural limits they were used to convey? In understanding these processes of othering Robert Bogdan argues "we have to look at those in charge – whether self appointed or officially – of telling us who deviants are and what they are like. Their versions of reality are presentations, people filtered through stories and world views... Presentations are artefacts of changing social institutions, organisational formations and world views."4 The time of the Victorian freakshow was a time of huge scientific discovery. With the rise of Darwinism, freakery was perhaps being used to establish biological normativity, to delimit what did and did not count as 'human'. Certainly this historical period was one when eugenics enjoyed a high international profile, with supporters on the political left and right arguing for organized control of the human gene pool, enforced sterilization of the feeble-minded and so forth. But in a sense, it doesn't matter. What we are talking about in these social processes is the assertion of 'acceptable' norms, i.e. what does and does not count as normal. Whether it's a life in the travelling show, being gawked and pointed at, or a life on television, being gawked and pointed at, the social political and cultural construction of what and what is not normatively acceptable is something that has been with us since before Victorian times.

I mention television to move the discussion away from a historical consideration of Victorian freak shows and eugenics, for there is a danger we get trapped in a historical abstraction and think in a self-congratulatory way that that was then, and that things have improved since those terrible times. And in part this is true. That processes of abjection and discrimination towards those deemed to be freaks happened is beyond doubt. But we have moved a long way from labelling people in these ways (in public discourse at least). Legislation or changing social attitudes have ensured (somewhat) that discrimination and attendant levels of stigma are deemed legally and socially unacceptable. Rightly, it is no longer possible to use a language of abnormality or imbecility when talking about physical disability or mental illness (indeed 'mental illness' has itself become a fraught term). But changing social mores and instituting legal frameworks has not functioned to rid contemporary society of the notion of the 'freak'. This is because the practices and processes of 'othering' remain largely unabated.

Take for example the ways in which mainstream media have represented issues of poverty and welfare, particularly how they have constructed the idea of 'poverty porn'. These programmes offer up a window on the 'freakshow' of life on welfare. Issues of deviance and stigma are bound up to a voyeuristic affirmation that for us, viewers in the mainstream, 'our lives' are not like those lives we see represented on the screen. In this way, poverty porn is used to define and delimit cultural expectations about work and welfare. It functions to communicate a message that a life on welfare is not somewhere that people want to go; the abjection of the poor is used as a timely reminder to make sure that we, viewers in the mainstream, keep on working, keep on striving, pay the mortgage, toe the line, for fear of being sacked and ending up on 'benefits street'. Tracy Jansen and Imogen Tyler demonstrate how these types of programmes develop a society-wide form of 'anti-welfare commonsense' where it becomes unproblematic to differentiate between a deserving and undeserving poor.5 That is to say, it facilitates the 'othering' of some groups of people, as establishing social processes that identify certain categories of people in society as less deserving of welfare than others.

Processes around the labelling of freaks and freakery are not about identifying the strange and the arcane (or even the profane). They are about setting the limits for what is 'acceptable', and 'normal' and for what people are expected to be (and not be). In modern times this means freaks and freakery are used to instil and install a normative need for the job, the car, the house and mortgage, the children, whilst continually buying more and more stuff that we don't really need in an endless cycle of consumption. What we really need are more 'freaks' — and lots of them.

Ewen Speed

1. Grosz, Elizabeth (1996) Intolerable Ambiguity: Freaks as/at the limit, in Rosemarie Garland Thomas (eds.) (1996) *Freakery: Cultural Spectacles of the Extraordinary Body*, London: New York University Press.

2. Foucault, Michel (2003) *'Society Must Be Defended': Lectures at the Collège de France, 1975–76*, trans. David Macey. New York: Picador.

3. Proctor, Robert (1988) *Racial Hygiene: Medicine under the Nazis*, London: Harvard University Press

4. Bogdan, Robert (1996) The Social Construction of Freaks, in Rosemarie Garland Thomson (1996) *Cultural Spectacles of the Extraordinary Body*, (eds.), London: New York University Press.

5. Jansen, Tracy and Tyler, Imogen (2015) 'Benefits broods': The cultural and political crafting of anti-welfare commonsense, *Critical Social Policy*, 35(4), 1-22.

THE DRAWINGS

PRINCE RANDIAN

Also known as 'The Snake Man', 'The Living Torso' and 'The Human
Caterpillar', Prince Randian was a Guyanese American performer who was
born with tetra-amelia syndrome, a condition characterized by the
complete absence of all four limbs. Prince Randian was brought to
the United States by P.T. Barnum in 1889. For his act he wore a one-piece
woollen body suit which gave him the appearance of a caterpillar and on
stage he would move himself about by wiggling his hips and shoulders. He
was best known for his ability to roll cigarettes with his lips, he spoke
Hindi, English, French, and German and was capable of painting, writing
and shaving himself by securing a razor in a wooden block. Married to a
woman known as Princess Sarah, Prince Randian fathered 4 daughters
and a son.

297 x 210 mm, Ink on Paper, 2014

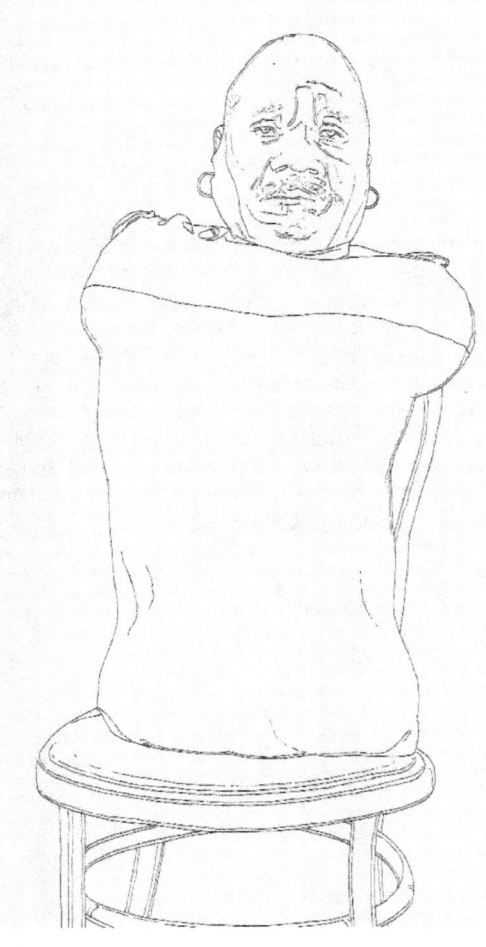

JO-JO THE DOG FACED BOY

Fedor Jeftichew was born in St. Petersburg, Russia in 1868 with the medical condition hypertrichosis lanuginosa. His father, Adrian, also had the same disorder and together they performed in French circuses. In 1884, Fedor signed a contract with P. T. Barnum who took him to Chicago and declared that Fedor had been captured by a hunter in the wilds of central Russia. A press conference was called where reporters were allowed to pull Fedor's hair so they could be assured of its authenticity. Barnum made a point of stressing Fedor's resemblance to a dog, explaining that when he was upset Jo-Jo would bark and growl, which he did in the show. Fedor would perform as many as 23 times a day and by 1886 he was earning up to US$500 a week.

297 x 210 mm, Ink on Paper, 2014

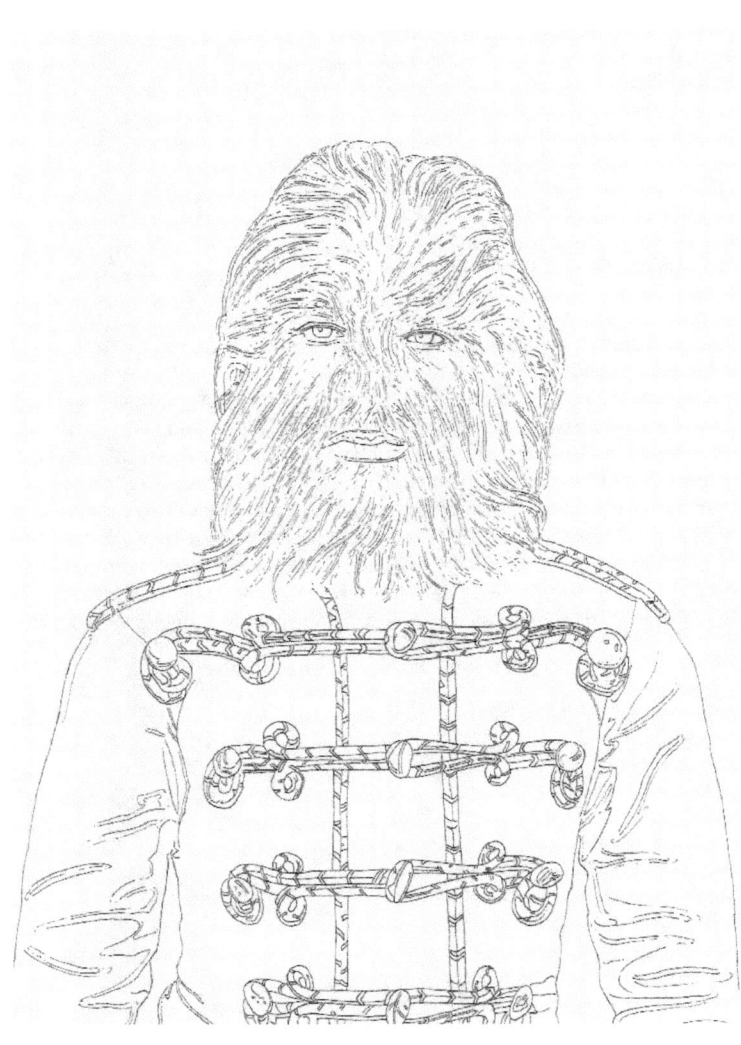

FRIEDA PUSHNIK

Frieda Pushnik's limbs were severed in the womb in 1923 as a result of a botched appendectomy on her mother. Her brother said the family never considered suing for malpractice and in a 1966 interview, Frieda explained that she never resented her condition, saying "I never said, 'Why me?' That would be a wasted emotion. You can ruin your life like that". As she grew her mother insisted she should do as much as possible for herself and by holding things between one small stump and her chin, she could eat, sew and crochet. In 1933, Robert L. Ripley asked her to appear at the World's Fair in Chicago where she undertook 5 minute demonstrations of typing, writing and sewing. She went onto appear in many shows for Ripley before moving to Barnum's as the 'Armless and Legless Wonder'.

297 x 210 mm, Ink on Paper, 2014

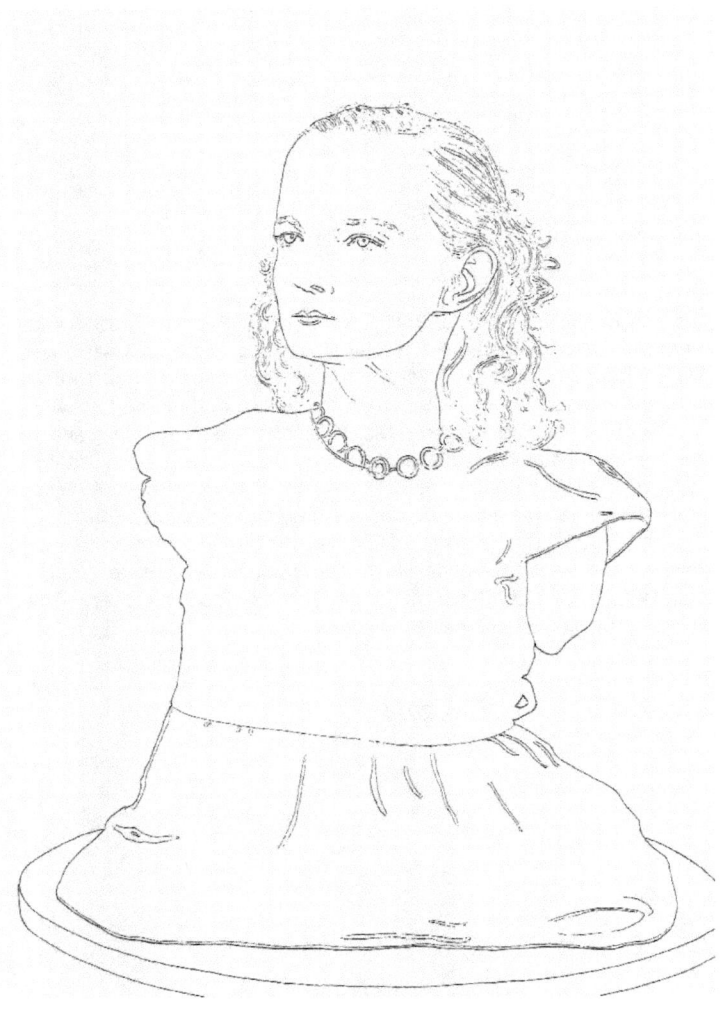

DAISY AND VIOLET HILTON

Fused at the pelvis, the Hilton twins were born in Brighton in 1908 and were the first conjoined twins in the UK to live for more than a few weeks. Mary Hilton, who helped deliver them, saw a commercial opportunity in the new-borns and effectively bought the girls from their mother. Along with her husband and daughter, Mary trained the girls in singing and dancing through physical abuse. The Hilton sisters then toured Britain in 1911 as 'The United Twins', before going on tour across the USA. When Mary Hilton died the girls were bequeathed to her daughter Edith Meyers. In 1931, the sisters sued Edith, gaining freedom from their contract and went into vaudeville as 'The Hilton Sisters' Revue'. Their popularity faded after the 1930s, and they took a job in a grocery store in Charlotte, North Carolina.

297 x 210 mm, Ink on Paper, 2014

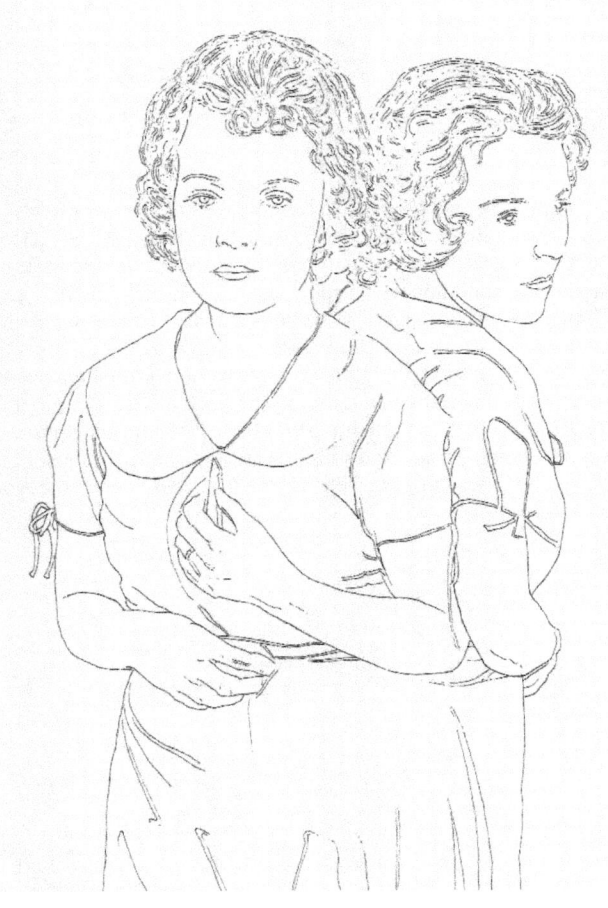

MARY ANNE BEVAN

Mary Anne Webster was born in London in 1874 and became a nurse. In 1903 she met and married Thomas Bevan and together they had 4 children. Shortly after their marriage Mary Anne developed acromegaly or "giantism", a condition which commonly has onset in middle-age. Acromegaly can cause facial distortions and abnormally large hands and feet as a result of the production of too much growth hormone. In 1914 Mary Anne's husband died suddenly leaving her without an income to support herself and their children, so she decided to make money from her condition. In 1920 Mary Anne was hired by Sam Gumpertz to appear in Coney Island's Dreamland sideshow, where she spent most of the remainder of her life performing as "the ugliest woman in the world" until her death in 1933.

297 x 210 mm, Ink on Paper, 2014

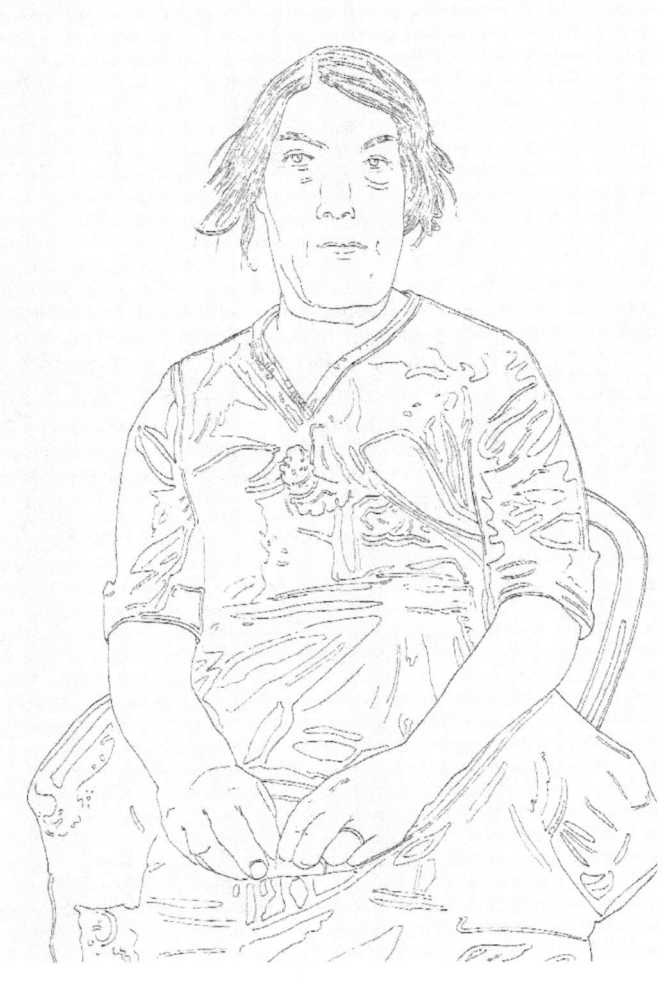

BARON PAUCCI

Peppino Margo was born in Sicily in 1894. At the age of 15 he survived the
Messina Earthquake, which appears to have been possible in part because
he was only 15 inches tall at the time. Following the earthquake Peppino
moved to the USA and began working for the Ringland Brothers Circus as
a side-show performer where he took the name 'Baron Paucci'. By the
time he was 29 years old he measured 27 inches tall, weighed 36 pounds
and was billed as the 'World's Smallest Perfect Man'. In 1931 Peppino
married Mavis Lane, who, at 5 foot tall was at the low end of 'normal' in
height. Sadly their marriage ended after a couple of years because of
Peppino's constant flirting with women who couldn't seem to resist
picking him up.

297 x 210 mm, Ink on Paper, 2014

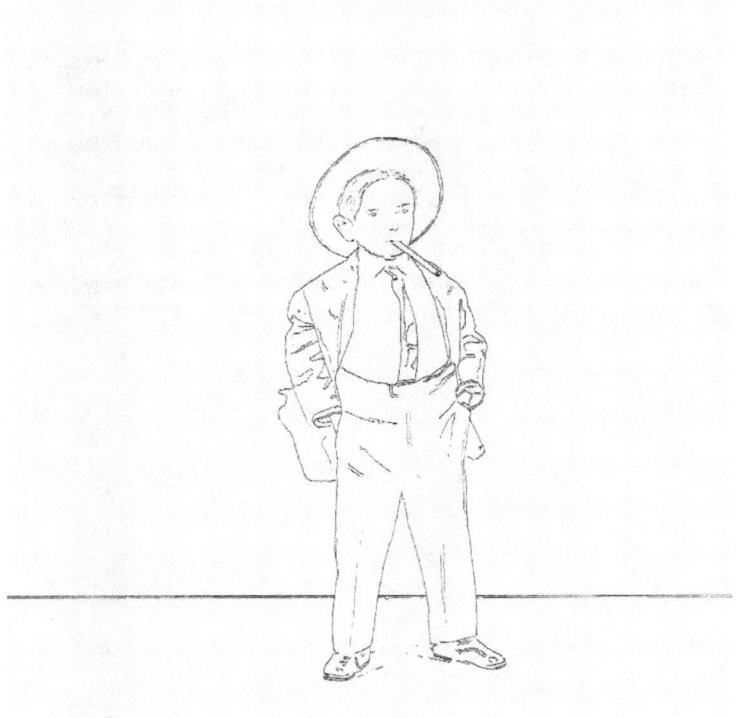

MADEMOISELLE GABRIELLE

Born in Basel, Switzerland in 1884, Gabrielle Fuller was born without legs, with her torso finishing just below the hip. She first joined the circus at the Paris Exposition in 1900 before travelling with the Ringling Brothers to appear in Coney Island's Dreamland Sideshow. Known as a 'half-lady' she also worked for Barnum and Bailey and undertook a short-lived career in vaudeville at the Hammerstein Theater in New York. Despite her condition Gabrielle always felt she was 'no less a woman' and many men are said to have found her attractive. She was married at least three times, first to a man with the surname of Hunter, then to John de Fuller and finally to an unknown German national, with her final years becoming a mystery.

297 x 210 mm, Ink on Paper, 2014

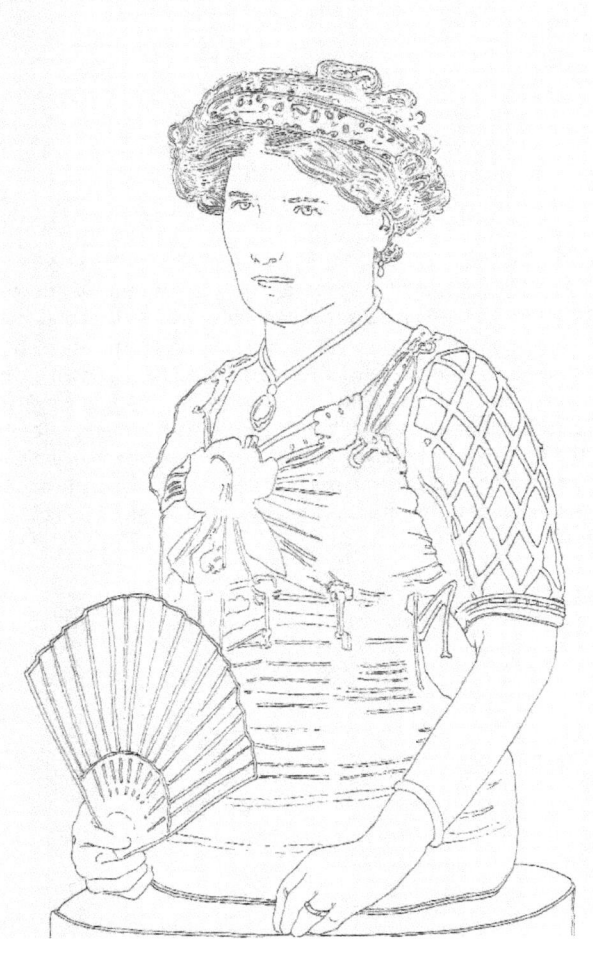

MYRTLE COBIN

Born in 1868 in Lincoln County, Tennessee with a condition known as dipygus, Myrtle Cobin had two separate pelvises from the waist down and four legs. Although she was able to move her two inner legs they were very small and considered too weak for walking on. Myrtle entered the sideshow circuit when she was 13 years old and was known as the "Four-Legged Girl from Texas". Her popularity grew to the point that other side-shows began creating four-legged gaffs (falsified performers) to fulfil the demand she created. At the age of 19 Myrtle married Clinton Bicknell and a year later became pregnant. She became very ill and had to have the pregnancy terminated, yet later went on to give birth to four daughters and a son.

297 x 210 mm, Ink on Paper, 2014

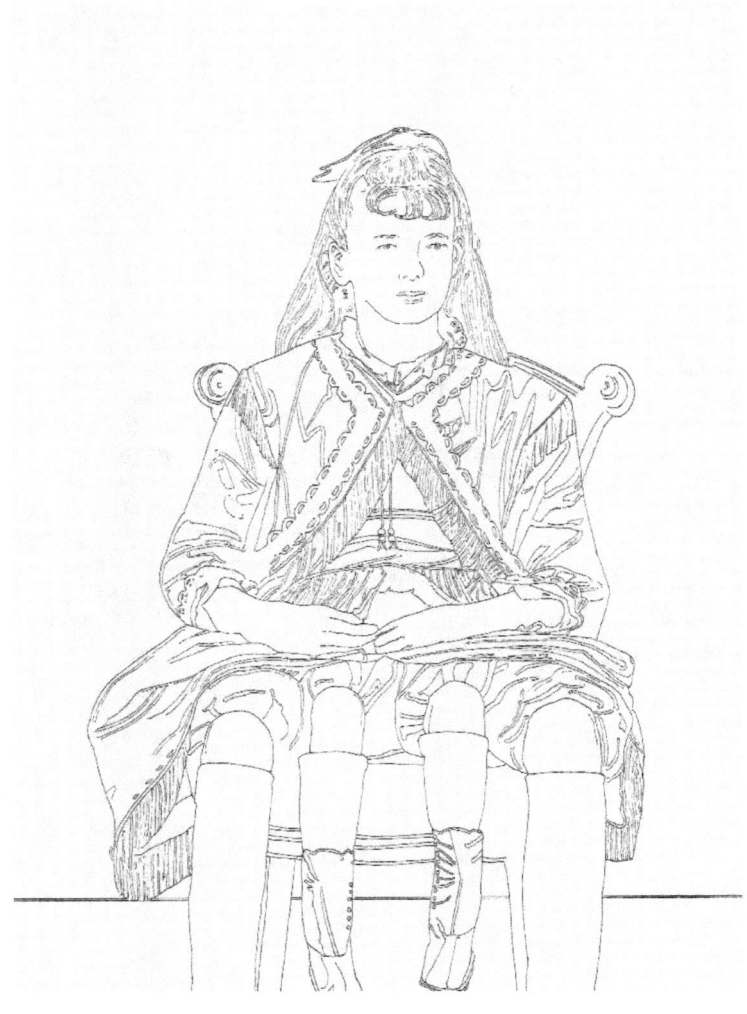

CAPTAIN ELVY CAMPBELL

Little is known about Captain Elvy other than he worked as a tattoo attraction in the 1940s. His tattoo was designed by "Sailor" George Fosdick and like many tattoos of the early 20th century it draws its inspiration from the maritime traditions which inform much naval art. Sailors were superstitious and specific tattoos were often employed to relieve anxieties over their beliefs; swallows held associations with a safe passage home, nautical stars with accurate navigation and crosses on the feet were seen to ward off sharks. Elvy's tattoos tie-in with this tradition and his body art was displayed at the Wallace Bros. sideshow in 1943. Unlike the majority of side-show performers who exhibited physical abnormalities, Elvy belonged to a group who were otherwise 'normal' but had either learned to do 'freakish' things with their bodies or inflicted extreme modifications upon them.

297 x 210 mm, Ink on Paper, 2014

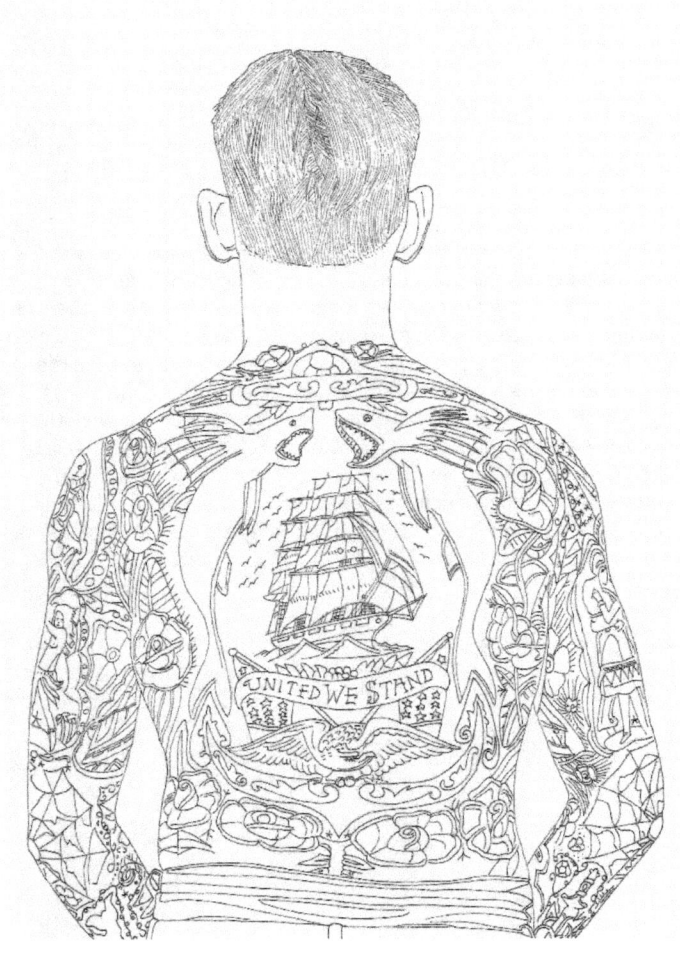

ALICE E. DOHERTY

Born in Minneapolis in 1887, to 'normal' parents, Alice lived with the rare
condition of hypertrichosis lanuginosa or 'dog-faced' hypertrichosis and
was covered all over in two-inch long, silky blonde hair, with the hair on
her head and face growing much longer. She began her exhibition career
when she was only 2 years old and by the age of 5 was touring the
American Midwest with her mother. Although only around 50 cases of
hypertrichosis lanuginosa have been reported worldwide since the Middle
Ages, Alice remained a minor figure on the turn-of-the-century side-show
circuit, never quite attaining the same fame and fortune as her
counterparts Fedor Jeftichew (Jo-Jo) and Stephan Bilgraski (Lionel).
Sometime between 1900 and 1910 Alice's family relocated to Dallas,
Texas, where she retired.

297 x 210 mm, Ink on Paper, 2014

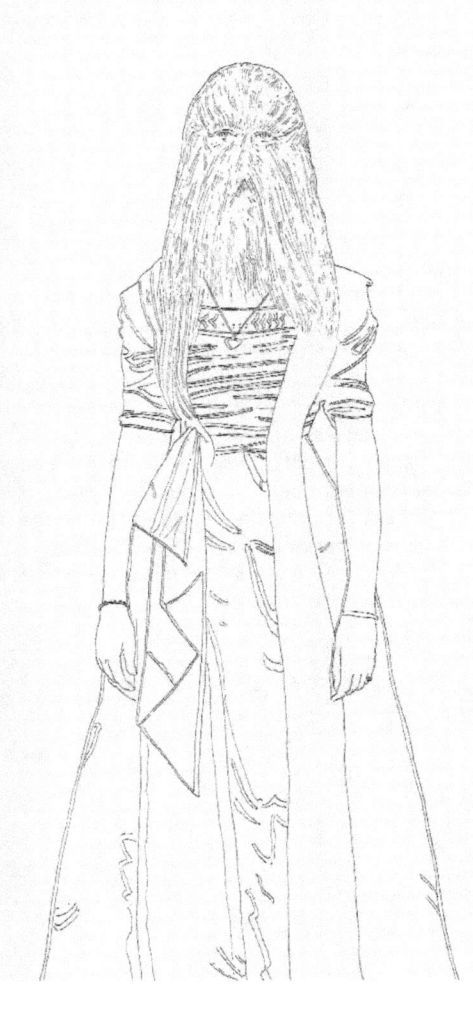

PIP AND FLIP

Sisters Jenny Lee and Elvira Snow were often publicized as coming "from the Yucatan" but were actually from Hartwell, Georgia, USA. They were born at the turn of the 20th century with a condition known as microcephaly, which results in an abnormally small cranium and brain after the head fails to grow in time with the face. The deformity often becomes more pronounced with age and produces impaired cognitive development. Jenny and Elvira both presented toddler-like personalities and worked in Coney Island as side-show performers where they were advertised as the 'Pinheads'. During the Great Depression they were said to be earning as much as $75 a week and in 1932 they featured in Tod Browning's 1932 film *Freaks*. Two years later Jenny Lee passed away, yet Elvira lived a long life and only died in 1976.

297 x 210 mm, Ink on Paper, 2014

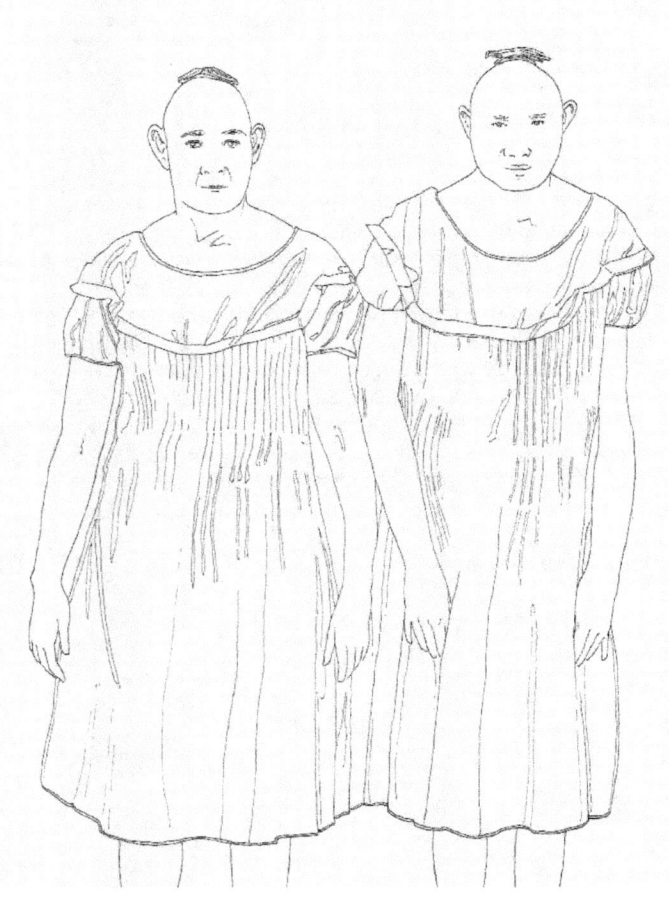

LUCIE ZARATE

Lucie Zarate was born in 1864 in San Carlos, Mexico. She is the first person in the World to have been identified as having majewski osteodysplastic, or primordial dwarfism. In 1876 she was measured at 20 inches tall, a height she had reached by the age of one. Then, when she was 17 Lucie was entered into the Guinness World Records as the 'lightest recorded adult', weighing just 4.7 pounds. Lucie moved to the United States when she was 12 where she was exhibited as a side-show performer in an act billed as the 'Fairy Sisters'. She later partnered with the American dwarf Francis Joseph Flynn. In 1890 the circus train she was travelling on became stranded in the snow covered Sierra Nevada mountains, where she caught hypothermia and died.

297 x 210 mm, Ink on Paper, 2014

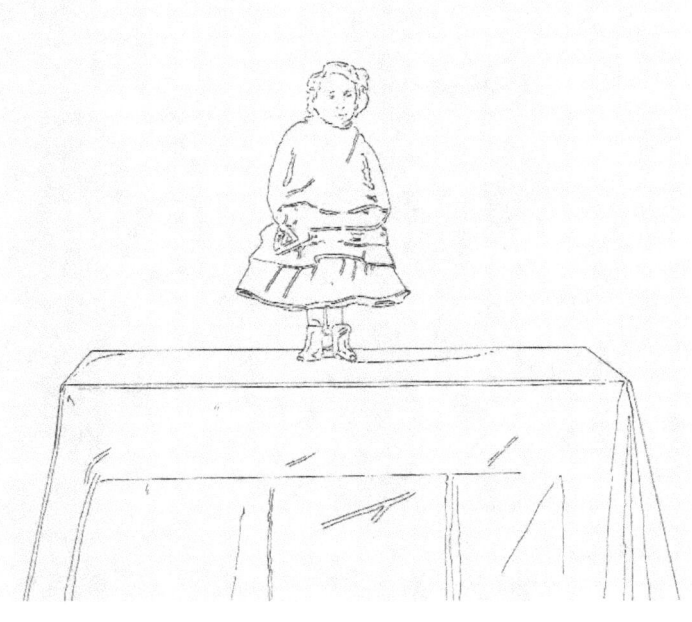

THANKS

Kaavous Clayton
Corrina Dunlea
Megan Hancock
Rebecca Kennedy
Cathy Lomax
John Priseman
Barbara Priseman
Ally Seabrook
Hannah Seabrook
Ewen Speed

The Denison Museum, Ohio
Gibberd Gallery, Harlow, UK
The Minories Art Gallery, Colchester, UK
The Transition Gallery, London